ARTEM KUDELIA PHD

Provocative Therapy

The Healing Power of Dark Humor

First edition

This book was professionally typeset on Reedsy.
Find out more at reedsy.com

Contents

Acknowledgments

I would like to express my gratitude to my psychology and psychotherapy teachers who have paved the way and established a solid foundation of knowledge. Furthermore, I extend my immense appreciation to patients, colleagues, friends, and all individuals who have directly or indirectly contributed to the writing of this book.

BONUS: Get Your Free Resources Now

I'm excited to share a **free eBook** and **exclusive access** to **psychological resources** with you. To get started, scan the QR code or visit psychemaster.com/provocative-therapy-the-healing-power-of-dark-humor

What You'll Get:

- **Free eBook**: Explore advanced psychotherapeutic techniques and approaches that complement the insights.
- **Interactive Learning**: Engage with exercises and quizzes to solidify your understanding of complex theories.
- **Latest Research**: Stay updated with the most recent findings in the field of psychotherapy and integrative therapy approaches.
- **Continuous Support**: Get consistent tips, strategies, and motivation to assist you in staying focused and excelling in your studies and practice.

Maximize your understanding of psychotherapy!

Introduction

In our opinion, the provocative psychotherapy approach is primarily influenced by the works of two American psychiatrists, Frank Farrelly and Milton Erickson.

While Farrelly focused on using sarcasm, humor, and irony when interacting with patients, Erickson's work included a wide range of techniques, not limited to the provocative approach alone, but also incorporating hypnosis. In this book, we will explore aspects of Erickson's work and analyze his methods of provoking patients. However, it is important to note that Erickson himself did not refer to his work as provocative. We will extensively delve into the application of Ericksonian hypnotic practices in books from the *Psychology and Psychotherapy: Theories and Practices Series*, specifically the *Hypnotherapy Fundamentals: Complete Guide* dedicated to the use of hypnosis in psychotherapy.

So, let's begin with Frank Farrelly.

Provocative Psychotherapy by Frank Farrelly

This form of psychotherapy originated in the 1960s. Farrelly, a young psychiatrist, initially practiced Carl Rogers' humanistic psychotherapy. However, through his own practice, he gradually developed a unique method that was different from others and formed his own understanding of effective psychotherapeutic work. Farrelly shared an epic story of when he began to have insights regarding the provocative approach. He was treating a married couple, where the husband had strong jealousy and believed his wife was cheating on him. She vehemently denied all accusations.

Farrelly was tasked with conducting a therapy session with the woman at her home, attempting to uncover the truth about their relationship. If she was not lying, then her husband could be diagnosed with paranoia. Frank went to the patient's home, conducted the therapy session, and noted that she behaved somewhat strangely. Her face reflected surprise and mild anxiety, and she answered questions directly. Eventually, she confessed that she had indeed been unfaithful. Frank didn't fully grasp what he was doing differently in his work that made the woman reveal what she hadn't said before.

Inspired, he returned to work, visited the restroom, and discovered that his white shirt was sticking out of his fly. It seemed that this unintentional criterion caused significant confusion for his patient and somehow made her more cooperative. He shared this incident with his colleagues, sparking hearty laughter. This incident allowed Frank to realize how creating confusion in psychotherapeutic work can influence a patient's behavior. This case was like the apple falling on Newton's head, leading to the understanding of the force of gravity.

Subsequently, he began experimenting with his ideas with different patients. In the first ten years of his practice, he worked extensively in a psychiatric clinic with psychotic patients, who often became the targets of his provocative experiments. Frank said that one day he entered the room with a group of schizophrenics who were busy on the floor.

He walked up to them and started teasing and making faces at them. They glanced at each other and began whispering anxiously, "Who let this mentally ill guy in here?" Undeterred, Frank continued to tease them. The schizophrenics asked him, "Who the hell are you?" Frank pointed to his badge, which displayed his psychiatrist credentials, and replied, "I'm a psychiatrist, and the fact that I have this identification means I'll leave the clinic today and go home, but it seems like you guys will stay here!"

In order to fully comment on Farrelli's work and explain the influence of his provocative method on patients' consciousness, it is worth digressing and commenting on some other topics.

Since Farrelli considered himself the father of humor in psychotherapy and, in my opinion, rightfully so, let us pay attention to the etymology of the word "humor" and trace its relationship to earlier times. Let us start with ancient Greece. It is from there that the word "humor" itself originated. In ancient Greece, thanks to Hippocrates, who is rightfully considered the "father of medicine," the doctrine of human temperament emerged. According to Hippocrates, a person's behavior is directly related to the balance of four bodily fluids that, in his opinion, circulate in the body - blood, yellow bile, black bile, and phlegm. Cholerics have an excess of yellow bile, which makes them impulsive. Phlegmatics have an excess of phlegm, which makes them calm and sluggish. Sanguines have an excess of blood, which makes them active and cheerful. Melancholics have an excess of black bile, which makes them sad and fearful.

In ancient Greek medicine, a person's state was described by the balance of these four bodily fluids and was called "humor." It was the proper balance of these fluids - the proper "humor" - that determined a person's health and well-being.

Different descriptions of the sense of humor can be found among various philosophers and thinkers of different eras. Let us mention some of them. For example, the Scottish philosopher D. Hume, in his essay, described a structural-logical process that can constitute a sense of humor. He referred to it as "the result of observing two or more illogical, incongruous, or absurd parts or circumstances considered to be united in one complex object or group."

In his book "The World as Will and Representation," A. Schopenhauer wrote that the two non-coinciding elements from which humor arises are a concept assimilated by us and a real object that "is conceived in this concept."

One of the first articles dedicated to humor in psychotherapy was found in Sigmund Freud's works. He named it "Humor and Its Relation to the Unconscious'' and published it in 1905. He hypothesized that humor is closely related to processes occurring in our unconscious. Like dreams, humor allows us to actualize those aspects of the unconscious that may be suppressed by the superego. Freud also divided humor into three categories, which he referred to as "joking," "comic," and "imitative." Humor creates a certain framework within which what is forbidden to express in other contexts and is prohibited by a person's superego can become acceptable and ecologically sound. Our aggressive and sexual tendencies, placed in a humorous context, can automatically be interpreted as socially acceptable.

Freud considered humor a specific "detour" through which our excessive psychic energy can be directed. According to Freud, humor is formally one of the sublimation processes of the psyche and a defense mechanism.

The English sociologist M. Malkay argues that humor serves to maintain social order by creating a special environment for expressing the contradictions that individuals encounter during socialization and active interaction with others. Malkay's theory largely coincides with Freud's views.

Evolutionary psychologist Geoffrey Miller, in his book "The Mating Mind," formulates and justifies an interesting theory stating that humor, in the context of natural sexual selection, served as a way to demonstrate intelligence. This makes humor in humans somewhat analogous to a "peacock's tail," indicating the individual's good genes.

To examine the structure of Frank Farrelly's work in more detail, we need to consider the main forms of transmitting humor that he uses in his provocative work. Most of the tools he employs are directly related to satire and are rhetorical figures of speech. These elements include irony, sarcasm, hyperbole, grotesqueness, allegory, and parody. In addition, Farrelly uses jokes, anecdotes, puns, and black humor. Let's describe them in more detail.

- **Irony**, translated from Ancient Greek as "pretense," is a satirical device in which the true meaning is concealed and contradicts the apparent observation. Irony is most often manifested through the contrast between verbal and non-verbal messages. For example, a phrase could be: "Oh yes, now you clearly understand me" (said when the interlocutor makes another mistake in a task). This phrase is spoken with a harsh, aggressive, or contemptuous tone. Farrelly is a master of playing with irony. For instance, when a patient tells him that they are going to achieve something, Farrelly asks, "Who?! You?!"—and does so with a manner and voice that clearly indicates his strong doubts about their ability to succeed in any way.

- **Sarcasm**, translated from Ancient Greek as "tearing of flesh," is one of the satirical techniques and is interpreted as a caustic mockery, the highest degree of irony, reinforced by an immediate intention to express the implied meaning. Sarcasm differs from irony in that it contains an expression of the highest degree of disapproval and even hatred. A brilliant example of sarcasm is Albert Einstein's phrase: "Two things are infinite: the universe and human stupidity. Of course, I'm not so sure about the universe." A notable example of sarcasm in Frank Farrelly's practice is the case of a woman who complained to him about not having enough energy to finish her dissertation. Frank began looking at her slight plumpness and pointed out why she didn't need to rush and could stay in place, gaining fat. He commented that men love fat women because they are faithful wives, and furthermore, they have a range of advantages, such as providing warmth in winter and shade in summer with their layers of fat.

- **Hyperbole** is a stylistic figure of explicit and intentional exaggeration aimed at emphasizing a specific meaning. Simple examples of hyperbole include phrases like "I've heard it a million times," "We've known each other for a hundred years," "Fast as lightning," and so on. Farrelly often uses hyperbole to exaggerate or diminish certain qualities of the patient's personality or behavior. Naturally, the use of hyperbole in provocative therapy goes hand in hand with irony and sarcasm.

- **Grotesque**, translated from French as "bizarre" or "comic," is a variety of artistic imagery that focuses on the bizarre and contrasting combination of the real and the fantastic, the comic and the horrible, the sublime and the grotesque, etc. A splendid example of literary grotesqueness is Hoffmann's novella "Little Zaches, nicknamed Zinnober." A direct example of the psychotherapeutic use of the grotesque by Frank Farrelly is the case he described when he had to start working with a very obese woman who underwent extensive physiological and psychological rehabilitation and weighed over 150 kilograms. When she entered the office, Farrelly said, "Hey, who let this Zeppelin dirigible in here?" The patient was initially embarrassed but then laughed and happily began working with the therapist. She had become so accustomed to people carefully trying to conceal their attitude toward her excessive weight that the grotesque honesty of the psychotherapist simply shifted her perspective.

- **Allegory**, translated from Ancient Greek as "metaphor," is a representation of an idea or concept through comparison with a specific artistic image or dialogue. It is often used in poetry, fables, and morality tales. Examples of allegories include "The world is a dove," "Fidelity is a dog," "Death is a skull," and so on. A vivid example of allegory in provocative therapy is the case of Frank Farrelly working with a young man who wanted to be a good leader. Frank took hold of his cheeks and began comparing him to a cherub, telling him that with such a charming and attractive appearance, he didn't need to worry about social achievements.

- **Parody**, a term consisting of two Ancient Greek words, "para" and "dia," translates as "beside, against" and "song," respectively. It involves creating a comic effect through intentional and deliberate imitation of certain traits of personality or behavior. The first notable example of parody in literature is the ancient work called "Batrachomyomachia" or "The Battle of Frogs and Mice," which parodies the style of Homer's "Iliad."

- **Joke** is a phrase or text that possesses humorous content. It may employ various rhetorical figures of speech and usually has a climax. Referring to various jokes by Farrelly, let's mention one remarkable example. By provoking a patient and pointing out their "worn-out" appearance, he commented, "Your eyes look like little holes in the snow, as if someone peed on it!"

- **Anecdote**, translated from Greek as "unpublished," is a brief narrative or retelling of an interesting incident. Anecdotes typically involve an unusual resolution intended to evoke laughter. In this case, we would like to provide an example from the work of therapist Stephen Gilligan, who often uses provocative elements in his therapy and seminars. We witnessed the following situation during the fourth day of a six-day generative trance training program led by Gilligan. Towards the end of the day, Stephen decided to liven up the audience a bit and said, "I would like to tell you an anecdote, but I'm not sure if you're mature enough for it." It's worth noting that there were over 250 therapists in the audience. All the program participants shouted back, "Stephen, we're listening!" He agreed to continue and shared the following anecdote: "Once upon a time, a cucumber, a mushroom, and a penis met at a bar. The cucumber started complaining that people pick and slice him, drizzle him with oil, and eat him. The mushroom complained that, in addition to everything else, he gets fried and cut into small pieces. When it was the penis's turn, he revealed that he usually faces an even more brutal fate. They put a plastic bag over him, stuff him into a red cave, and repeatedly slam his head against the ceiling until he throws up!" Half of the audience burst into uproarious laughter, while the other part froze in silent shock due to the unexpected semantic range of the anecdote. In our observation, the use of such provocative elements in education significantly enhances the quality of material assimilation and, when properly employed, can greatly enhance the effectiveness of both therapy and learning in general.

- **Pun**: A rhetorical and literary device that uses different meanings of a word or different words and phrases in the same context.

- **Dark humor** often uses cynicism to ridicule death, diseases, traumas, pathologies, and other grim subjects that people usually don't like to joke about. It can employ irony, sarcasm, and other rhetorical figures of speech, but in a much harsher manner. The term itself originated in French and was popularized by André Breton, who compiled the "Anthology of Black Humor" in 1939. In Frank Farrelly's practice, we observed several instances where he compared patients to the well-known patient Helen Keller, who was blind, deaf, and mute. In other cases, Frank would directly comment on the patient's symptom as fatal, leading to worse consequences, and attribute it to poor heredity, suggesting that psychotherapy alone cannot yield positive results.

- **Oxymoron**, translated from ancient Greek as "witty foolishness," is a figure of speech that combines contradictory concepts, creating a combination of incongruity. Examples may include "joyful sadness," "living dead," "dead souls," and so on.

Farrelly Factors

Frank Farrelly conducted various seminars worldwide dedicated to the provocative psychotherapy method for about 50 years. His students often asked Frank how reproducible his psychotherapy method was. Frank usually liked to joke and said that he believed only 400 million people were capable of provocative psychotherapy. He also enjoyed sharing a story about one of his seminars in Germany, where a German attendee asked him about the main personal characteristic necessary to effectively conduct provocative psychotherapy. Frank replied, "Write it down!" All of his German students eagerly reached for their pens, ready to jot down the "secret knowledge" from Frank Farrelly. To their surprise, he said, "To be a truly good provocative psychotherapist, you need to be born Irish!" As we can see from his responses, Farrelly not only practiced provocative forms of psychotherapy but also had a provocative communication style in general.

Some of Farrelly's students from the Netherlands—Jaap Hollander, Graham Davies, and René Dubois—modeled his behavior during provocative psychotherapeutic work. Based on their modeling, they identified key rules, strategies, and patterns that they believed were most characteristic of his behavior in the psychotherapy process. In total, they came up with seven categories that encompassed 39 behavioral elements.

Categories

1. Regular therapist behavior. This refers to what the therapist consistently does during the psychotherapeutic process.
2. Cause-and-effect behavior. These are specific, fixed reactions of the therapist to certain patient actions.
3. Alternative means of provocation. These are specific forms of behavior that the therapist uses intermittently, rather than consistently.
4. Reactions to patient comments about problems.
5. Reactions to patient comments about self-esteem.
6. Internal processes accompanying Frank Farrelli during provocative work sessions.
7. Strategic actions.

Regular Therapist Behavior

Physical contact support: During psychotherapeutic sessions, Farrelli often touches the patient. This can involve touching their hands, patting their shoulders, wiping the patient's tears (symbolically or actually, if present), and touching and holding the patient's chin. Overall, Frank frequently enters the patient's personal space. If the patient avoids these touches, he repeats them after a while.

Use of different intonations: Depending on the patient and the topic being discussed, Farrelli's intonation can vary significantly. The following types of intonations can be observed:

- ***Playful***: This tone of voice is often used to start an interview. For example, Frank jokingly refers to a patient named Alexander as "the emperor" and asks what his specific problem is.
- ***Hypnotic***: With this tone of voice, Farrelli starts stating various therapeutic truths.
- ***Pretend-upset***: Farrelli may use this tone of voice when he notices that what he is doing or saying is disliked. Other applications of this type of voice are also possible.
- ***Pompous***: We have noticed that Farrelli tends to use a pompous tone of voice when commenting on his grandiose and absurd ideas about the patient's future.
- ***Condescending***: This tone of voice is often used when the patient's shortcomings come into focus.

Use of nonverbal mirroring: Quite often, during work with a patient, Frank mimics their postures, gestures, tone, intonation, and other nonverbal signals. As far as we could ascertain, he does not do this intentionally. This phenomenon seems to occur naturally during communication. In cases where intentional mirroring of nonverbal communication does occur, it takes on a mocking and parodic character.

Use of anecdotes, jokes, and comedic stories: Depending on the patient and their case, Farrelli may share anecdotal stories that are relevant to the situation. An interesting aspect is Frank's feedback regarding how he accumulates jokes for therapy. When reading a book, he highlights particularly interesting and humorous moments. If he hears a good joke in real life or in a video, he envisions how that joke can be applicable during a provocative therapy session with a patient.

Complete focus on the patient: Farrelli strives to ignore other stimuli unrelated to the work. He may also speak firmly to the patient, emphasizing that while he is working with them, they should be focused on him. If someone in the audience disturbs him, he can authoritatively request silence. Sometimes, the demand for silence in the audience can take on a provocative character. For instance, we have seen Frank speak sternly to a participant in the group who was disrupting the silence, warning that if they didn't calm down, he would approach and sit on their face!

Lack of actual assistance to the patient: It implies that a provocative psychotherapist should not give the patient serious advice on how to be or what to do. Here, we must emphasize the non-directive quality of their work. Behind the strange, sarcastic, grotesque, and foolish advice lies the intention to push the patient towards independent decision-making and conclusions. In this sense, Frank Farrelly's style of work can be quite similar to Milton Erickson's approach.

Lack of a clear plan for working with the patient: A provocative psychotherapist does not have a clear idea of where they want to lead the patient. There is no clear plan or goal. Actions are intuitive and oriented towards verbal and nonverbal feedback from the patient. If the therapist's behavior indicates that they do have some plan, it often has an absurd connotation.

Easy distraction from the topic and absurd focus of attention: Farrelly often switches from one topic to another, ignoring the completion of the previous one. He frequently elaborates on absurd and insignificant details. He may indifferently comment on what the patient considers important and, conversely, discuss as highly significant what the patient deems irrelevant. There may be examples where, in the middle or towards the end of a session, Frank clarifies with the patient what exactly their problem is.

Provocation of desired behavior: The term "provocare" translates from Latin as "revealing, eliciting." However, this "challenge" of behavior in provocative psychotherapy takes on a non-directive and quite often an inversive form. Behind the teasing lies the intention to evoke self-confidence; behind sarcastic remarks about flaws lies the desire to discover energy to eliminate them; and behind irony regarding certain personality traits lies the intention to create self-awareness in the specific personal context of the patient, and so on. Here, one can recall a phrase from Goethe's work spoken by Mephistopheles: "I am part of that power which eternally wills evil and eternally works good."

Causal-dependent Behavior

Eliciting emotions in the patient: Farrelly believes that one of the main goals of provocative therapy is to evoke various emotions in the patient. The spectrum of emotions can be very diverse, including joy, anger, sadness, embarrassment, and so on. Throughout the therapy, Farrelly explores the patient's reactions to various topics. If the reaction is strong, he continues to comment on the topic; if it is weak, he may start looking for other points to focus attention on. Farrelly has a specific list of main topics that are frequently used in provocative therapy, such as male-female relationships, sex, politics, religion, and others. Each patient may have their own vulnerable areas that need to be discovered during the therapeutic process.

Acting contrary to the patient's wishes: If a patient insists on one thing, do the opposite. If they want the topic of discussion to be changed, keep it unchanged. If they want the therapist to stop, it becomes an excellent command to continue doing what the therapist is currently doing.

Noting and commenting on strong nonverbal reactions from the patient: Farrelly observes strong nonverbal reactions from the patient, may exaggerate their description, and asks the patient if they understand what is happening to them at the moment.

Detailing information: When a patient utters abstract and vague phrases, Farrelly asks them to clarify and provide a more detailed description. Sometimes, for the purpose of obtaining detailed information from the patient, Farrelly uses a provocative trick. Instead of asking for clarification, he starts uttering presumed possible details himself. However, he does it provocatively and absurdly, which the patient often disagrees with and responds to by providing the actual necessary information.

The use of trance work: Sometimes, during the interaction with a psychotherapist, the patient may enter a light trance state and appear "suspended." Farrelly takes advantage of these moments to utter certain therapeutic truths, such as "Deep down, you must know," "We know that there is some solution," "There are things you can truly change," and so on. Thus, he often employs cliché phrases that hold inherent truth and are difficult to resist due to their statements of obvious facts. In this pattern, conventional provocation is not employed; only resourceful statements are used.

Serious and non-provocative approach to significant traumas: When Farrelly hears patients' stories about the loss of loved ones or severe illnesses, he immediately adopts a serious tone and occasionally expresses condolences. If the death of a loved one or a serious illness is the main theme of therapy, his approach becomes gentle and delicate. Farrelly avoids using harsh and rigid provocations regarding these topics.

Mirroring incongruent messages: When a patient conveys an incongruent message, verbally stating that something is important while non-verbally indicating the opposite, Farrelly responds by demonstrating similar behavior. For instance, if a patient speaks with a lethargic and apathetic tone, emphasizing the significance of something, Farrelly responds in a similar intonation, acknowledging that it is indeed very important.

Alternative means of provocation

Interrupting and cutting off the patient: Farrelly frequently employs this pattern. Sometimes he interrupts the patient right at the beginning of their reasoning or simply doesn't allow them to finish their sentence. Rarely does he grant the patient the opportunity to speak at length. The underlying philosophy of this pattern is that in the practice of provocation, politeness and etiquette should not be observed.

Parodying and mimicking the patient: Farrelly exaggerates certain types of patient behavior, mimicking them in a comedic manner. At times, the mimicry may even transition into a small theatrical performance for a solo actor.

Demonstrating how the patient's behavior can influence others: This pattern is naturally executed in an exaggerated, comedic manner. If the patient behaves aggressively, Farrelly may pretend to be frightened and ask them not to hit him, shielding his face with his hands as a protective gesture. In the case of excessive sexual behavior exhibited by a female patient, he may play the role of a man struggling to restrain his sexual urges, and so on.

Incorrect and unexpected interpretations of the patient's behavior and reactions: The more absurd and strange these interpretations are, the better. Sometimes the comments may have no relevance to the actual topic at hand. In other cases, Farrelly may propose something diametrically opposed to the real situation.

Strange, unconvincing, and foolish attempts to refute the patient's comments about any achievements: Farrelly starts presenting various strange arguments to support the notion that success is not truly success. He may suggest that it could lead to negative consequences or simply be greatly exaggerated. All refutations are often illogical and far-fetched.

Discrediting the patient's belief in the positive feedback they receive from others in response to their behavior: Farrelly may begin listing peculiar reasons why this is not the case and why the patient needs to change their perspective on the current state of affairs.

Asking the patient to repeat strong statements: If a patient makes any statement about themselves or life, Farrelli may pretend not to understand or misunderstand, thereby provoking them to repeat the phrase.

Dramatization and exaggeration of fantasies, fabrications, and inventions: To illustrate his point, Farrelli doesn't just tell a story; he turns it into a small, one-actor theater. During the performance, he may associate with various characters from history and speak from the perspective of each character.

Reactions to patients comments about problems

Encouragement of problem behavior: Farrelli focuses his attention on the various real shortcomings of the patient and tries to persuade them to maintain and preserve these shortcomings. For example, if Farrelli learns that the patient is living off other people who help them, he starts convincing the patient that they are engaging in very advantageous behavior and that they should choose friends who allow them to take advantage.

Offering surrealistic solutions: Farrelli constantly suggests strange, absurd, and surrealistic solutions to current problems and tasks. As he comments on these solutions, he often proposes problematic and environmentally unfriendly types of behavior and reactions. If the patient starts resisting, Farrelli continues to insist on his proposal and sometimes tries to present it as the only possible option.

Offering absurd interpretations: This point is very similar to the previous one. However, in this case, various strange interpretations of what is happening, what has happened, and what may happen to the patient are offered rather than solutions.

Minimizing the magnitude of the problem compared to other more favorable life factors: Farrelli may provide comments regarding areas of the patient's life where things are going well and begin to persuade them that nothing needs to be changed because of that. The comparisons are often absurd and come across as silly.

Reactions to the patient's comments about self-esteem

Exaggeration and caricature of negative self-esteem in one's state or behavior: If the patient tells Farrelli that things may not be going exactly as they would like, he may start proving to them that they are already at rock bottom with no way out. Naturally, absurd interpretations are used to support his opinion.

Exaggeration and caricature of negative perceptions of one's appearance: This pattern is almost a replica of the previous one, but the focus shifts to the perception of one's body and overall appearance.

Exaggeration of existing cultural stereotypes: Farrelli particularly enjoys playing on the exaggeration of stereotypical cultural perceptions of male and female images. He may use exaggerations of religious, cultural, and political stereotypes.

Internal processes accompanying Frank Farrelli during provocative therapy sessions

Entering a resourceful humorous state: This state allows for tuning into the desired provocative wave in communication and generating the necessary psychotherapeutic interventions.

Perceiving the patient as a close friend and maintaining warm feelings towards them: No matter how harsh the sarcasm coming from the provocative psychotherapist towards the patient may be, it should stem from a friendly attitude and acceptance.

Engaging internal mentors: During the session, one can imagine what people whom they consider their mentors in various aspects of life would say about the patient. A good frame that creates the necessary state for implementing this pattern could be a question to oneself: "What would one of my acquaintances say about this person?" and so on.

Visualizing internal monitors: Farrelli, during his interaction with the patient, can visualize various monitors next to him that offer different ways of communicating with the patient and different options for guiding provocative work.

Strategic actions

Shifting responsibility for events from the patient to circumstances and vice versa: If the patient blames themselves for something, start reproaching the world, society, other people, and circumstances. If they start blaming others, lay all the blame on them. Naturally, this is done in a tragicomic and absurd manner.

Taking one side in a conflict the patient comments on: It is possible to support both the patient's side and the opposing side. The provocative psychotherapist begins to favor the side whose defense can evoke more emotions and protest reactions from the patient. A very good example could be an existing conflict between the patient's parents.

Demanding the patient entertain the psychotherapist: Farrelli often emphasized in his seminars that "the patient's main task is to entertain the psychotherapist!"

Exhibiting behavior wilder and more absurd than the patient's: For instance, when Farrelli worked with an eight-year-old child who burped in his presence, he started burping even louder and more intensely.

Archetypal Foundation of Provocative Work - Trickster and the Sacred Fool Myths

Studying Frank Farrelli's work reveals that his method of therapy is, in many ways, a fascinating "underbelly" of many other forms of psychotherapy, particularly humanistic therapy, in which Farrelli began his career as a psychotherapist. Provocative therapy demonstrates how many beliefs prevalent in the psychotherapeutic context, when turned upside down, can produce not only a good but even a better effect. This may give rise to the humorous belief that the competence of a provocative therapist is a form of competent incompetence in conducting the psychotherapeutic process.

Here, we are reminded of Mephistopheles' line from Goethe's work: "I am part of that power which eternally wills evil and eternally works good." This quote indeed aligns well with the philosophy of provocative work, although it requires some additional clarifications. Farrelli commented in his seminars that he perceives provocative therapy as a type of exorcism, where the patient's neurosis is "expelled" through mockery and teasing. Farrelli expressed his belief that "the devil does not tolerate mockery of himself." He also emphasized that it is the symptom itself that is being ridiculed, not the patient. And indeed, a person who can afford to joke about their symptoms is at least halfway towards recovery.

Farrelli also introduced an interesting metaphor into his work, referring to provocative therapy as a form of "devil's advocate" work. In this case, we see not literal mockery but rather the therapist adopting a role where they comically begin to defend the symptom to the patient, persuading them to preserve and keep it. The foundation of this approach lies primarily in the intentional incongruence of the message, where part of the verbal message clearly reflects the defense of the symptom, while non-verbal bodily and auditory messages reflect the comedy and grotesque nature of the message. Not to mention that the verbal rational arguments themselves are often quite absurd. Thus, the psychotherapist begins to reveal and mock the shadowy, unconscious aspects of the patient's personality through their behavior.

The projection of the shadow from the depths of the unconscious onto the therapist's behavior leads to the initiation of possible psychodynamic processes. After all, a symptom exists and remains invulnerable only when its key meaning pattern is deeply hidden in the unconscious. In this case, a good metaphor can be the fairy tale character Koschei the Immortal, whose death is hidden in an egg that is far away from him. Additionally, by exploring Farrelli's work, we can find a profound underlying intention—to turn everything inside out. If a person wants to get rid of a particular behavior, persuade them to maintain the same pattern. If a person praises their own merits, convince them that they are not particularly significant. If a person believes they are guilty of something, start convincing them of the correctness of their opinion, but do it in a tragicomic manner.

In Paul Radin's book with commentaries by Carl Jung and Karl Kerényi, a very interesting mythological character belonging to the mythology of the Winnebago Indians is described, whose behavior somewhat resembles the philosophy of provocative work. This deity is called the Trickster. Radin's book dedicated to the Trickster presents a large number of myths about him. These myths are quite strange, and their plots may be incomprehensible to the Western mentality. However, if we read a certain number of these myths, we will discover a very interesting meta-meaning that permeates them.

Paul Radin

In various myths, the Trickster appears in different forms. In one myth, he is a man, in another, a woman; in one, he is a hero, in another, a criminal; in one, he saves someone from death, while in another, he becomes a killer. This list can go on, but the essence remains the same. The Trickster embodies philosophical notions of non-duality, which are characteristic not only of Native American Indians but also of Indian sages.

In the ancient Indian treatise "Bhagavad Gita," it is mentioned that the person who attains a state of non-dual mind is saved. The state of non-duality is the simultaneous perception of opposites as parts of a whole, which allows a person to perceive the world in its true form. We believe that it was Hindu concepts of non-duality, or teachings closely related to these concepts, that influenced Carl Jung in creating his idea of the existence of the archetype of the Self in personal and collective unconsciousness.

Carl Jung

In one of his books, Carl Jung provides a direct definition of this archetype, stating that "the Self is the union of opposites." True opposites can be perceived as masculine and feminine, light and dark, manifest and hidden, and so on. Each individual opposition can be embodied in a separate archetype, which itself may consist of individual opposites.

In Jungian psychology, the Trickster archetype is often perceived as a variation of the Wise Old Man archetype. In my opinion, it also has a more abstract nature and serves as a kind of meta-archetype, representing the transformation of one archetype into its diametrical opposite. Jung called the process of transitioning from one thing to its diametrically opposite enantiodromia, which he considered a key vector of natural transformation in the individual's personality.

We believe that the process of enantiodromia is an integral

part of the Trickster's archetypal function, both as a mythological figure and as an abstract process. There is a belief that the Trickster archetype finds its embodiment in various gods or heroes in different mythological structures and exists in almost every cultural tradition. All the embodied figures convey the key qualities inherent in the Trickster archetype.

Most often, the image of the Trickster hero embodies demonic and comedic traits, possessing the qualities of a trickster and prankster. It can be a god, a human, or an anthropomorphic animal. In the process of solving the challenges that arise during the development of the myth, the Trickster violates various rules of a certain property and eventually finds a distinctive solution to the existing challenge.

At this moment, an analogy arises with the provocative form of psychotherapy, which violates numerous rules existing in other psychotherapeutic methods and often generates solutions that are so original that they can be awe-inspiring. In my opinion, in the process of interacting with the patient on a deep level, a provocative psychotherapist associates with the archetype of the Trickster and its transformative psychic energy, capable of introducing new original solutions.

An interesting parallel to the image of the Trickster in Winnebago Indian mythology is represented by the thunder deity Heyoka in Sioux-Dakota myths. He is the patron of hunting. Heyoka embodies the paradoxical nature of the Trickster's image and all the processes and phenomena inherent in it. There are mythological descriptions that depict a joyful Heyoka as crying heavily, while when he is saddened, he laughs. Heat affects him as if it were cold, and vice versa.

Once again, we can draw a cross-reference to the provocative nature of the work, which, according to Farrell, unlike other methods of psychotherapy, does not fight against the resistance of the patient but instead creates it, with the aim of using the energy of this resistance to transform the symptom.

The Sioux people believe that after thunder, the world begins to renew itself, and it is appropriate to welcome it with joy. People who assume the role of Heyoka in the tribe are often referred to as clowns or madmen because they perform acts that are contrary to what is natural and expected. Once again, we can recognize Farrell's behavior in these descriptions. Indeed, his behavior is often perceived by people as clowning and a manifestation of madness. However, this is not the only role he can assume within the context of psychotherapeutic practice.

Dr. Walker, an American anthropologist, describes the ceremony dedicated to Heyoka as follows: "When someone seeks a vision and sees lightning or Thunderbird, such a person must subsequently mimic Heyoka through clowning and absurdity in words and actions. The special action he must perform is to snatch meat from a boiling pot with bare hands and offer it to someone."

Let's provide examples of how the Trickster archetype is embodied in various other mythological figures:

- Little St. Martin in Basque mythology
- Loki and Odin in Germanic and Scandinavian mythology
- Hephaestus, Hermes, and Odysseus in Ancient Greek mythology
- Azazel in Levantine mythology
- Baron Samedi and Papa Legba in Voodoo mythology
- Reynard the Fox from Dutch folklore
- Ivan the Fool from Russian folklore
- Nasreddin Hodja, from the folklore of Central Asia and other

countries;

- Uncle Tompa from Tibetan folklore
- Puss in Boots from French folklore
- Sun Wukong, the Monkey King, from Chinese mythology
- Kitsune, Susano-o, and Kappa in Japanese mythology
- Iktomi Heyoka in Lakota mythology
- Amaguk in Inuit mythology
- Anansi the Spider among West African peoples;
- Hare among Bantu ethnic groups
- Tjank or Tokoloshe among the Zulu people;
- Set in Ancient Egypt
- Figaro from the folklore of the Spanish people;
- Br'er Rabbit from US folklore
- Hershele Ostropoler from Jewish folklore
- Coyote (Huehuecoyotl) in Aztec mythology.

In my opinion, these mythological and cultural figures, to varying degrees, reflect the meanings contained within the Trickster archetype and can be perceived as symbolic prototypes of provocative forms of psychotherapeutic work.

The stories of these characters can also be used as metaphors in teaching provocative therapy. This form of education is highly significant as it focuses on the perception of information primarily through the activity of the right hemisphere of the brain, which processes the perceived world through abstract symbols, unlike the left hemisphere, which prefers clear and detailed information. It is the activity of the right hemisphere that is capable of creating a sense of flow during the practice of provocative therapy, where therapeutic interventions arise easily and naturally, closely connected to verbal and non-verbal messages coming from the patient to the psychotherapist.

In my opinion, this sense of flow becomes accessible only when the psychotherapist grasps the abstract core of the work itself, which can be understood by studying myths, legends, and folklore related to various manifestations of the Trickster archetype.

Provocative Group Psychotherapy

At times, Farrelly demonstrated examples of his work with a group during his seminars. The technique of provocative therapy itself did not undergo significant changes, but certain elements of this applied practice are worth noting.

In our view, a group for this form of therapy should be limited in terms of the number of participants, with an optimal range of 4–8 individuals. And based on our practice, it's closer to 4 rather than 8. A smaller number of people, less than 4, does not create the full effect of group psychotherapy, where each patient can create multiple transferences onto their peers. A larger number, more than 8 individuals, is undesirable as the provocative approach relies heavily on the intensive work of the psychotherapist, and their attention simply won't be sufficient for all participants, or they will be spread too thin to create the necessary therapeutic effect. The optimal duration for the group session is 45–90 minutes. With an increased number of participants, it is better to slightly extend the time.

Initially, the therapist starts by introducing various minor provocations to the group participants while carefully observing their non-verbal reactions. It is quite possible that a provocation directed at one participant elicits a strong response from another. General phrases aimed at provoking the entire group may also be uttered. At times, the therapist may spontaneously switch from one patient to another. After working with one patient, they may receive feedback on the topic being addressed and then switch to another topic. Let us formulate the key rules of group provocative therapy.

Rules of Group Provocative Therapy

1. Therapist takes on the majority of the activity.
2. Therapist constantly switches from one patient to another.
3. The amount of time dedicated to each patient can vary significantly, ranging from a brief phrase to a dialogue lasting up to 5 minutes.
4. Provocations should ideally engage not only the targeted patient but also others. The aim is to create interventions that can provoke multiple individuals or even the entire group simultaneously.
5. It is possible to intertwine the meanings of conversations with different patients logically and provocatively. Some patients can be used as instruments to provoke others.
6. Strive to allocate approximately equal time to each patient.
7. Capture the sense of flow and act intuitively, shifting from one person to another.

During one of his seminars, Farrelly shared that he had previously applied group provocative therapy to working with groups of criminal psychopaths in prison. One participant in such a group once told Frank that he was cool. Frank asked him, "What makes you say that?" The prisoner replied that he behaved terribly in their presence but was sincere in his communication and did not burden them with lofty "humanistic crap."

Provocative Coaching

Farrelly commented on how his student from the Netherlands, Jaap Hollander, along with some colleagues, organized an educational program specifically dedicated to provocative coaching work. Frank himself did not differentiate between regular provocative psychotherapy and coaching practice, stating, "To me, they are one and the same." Nevertheless, if we specifically consider the philosophy of coaching, which is primarily focused on assisting in achieving future goals rather than therapeutic exploration of the past, there are certain changes in provocative work that, in my opinion, should be taken into account. The following focal points should become the focus areas for provocative work in coaching.

Provocative Attention Foci for Coaching

1. **Future orientation**: The provocative therapist directs the vector of provocation more toward future events.
2. **Working with the inferiority complex**: This focus emphasizes the deliberate creation of an inferiority complex that can serve as energy for goal attainment.
3. **Coach as "devil's advocate"**: This focus guides the therapist's efforts to present all the advantages and benefits

that can be gained if the patient abandons their goal.

4. **Provocative metaphors of achievement**: The therapist employs various absurd metaphors of goal attainment. For example, the therapist might say to the patient, "Simpleton Ivan started by lying on the stove. Maybe you should find one and lie on it for a while too?"
5. **Multiple false goals**: Operating within this focus, the therapist begins to suggest numerous minor, insignificant additional goals to divert the patient's attention. Naturally, this is done in a comedic manner to make it appear as theatrical absurdity to the patient.

Provocative Drama

In the course of our practice, we have developed a highly interesting way of applying provocative work within a group setting, which, to the best of our knowledge, Farrelly has never used in his practice. The essence and philosophy of provocative work itself remain unchanged. However, different group members can participate in the actual dramatic representation of verbal provocation for the purpose of provoking reactions. Initially, the therapist may work in the usual provocative style. However, as the context of the symptom is understood, they begin to model the situation itself through the use of substitutes playing different roles. The therapist directs the scene, providing instructions on where each performer should stand, what posture to assume, and what to comment on. If necessary, the therapist may ask the patient to improvise within the given thematic context. Sometimes, the patient themselves can also actively participate in the provocative drama. Therefore, provocative work incorporates structural and technical elements from other forms of dramatic psychotherapy, such as Jacob Moreno's psychodrama and Virginia Satir's "family sculpture."

Advantages of this approach include

1. Visualizing the role within the problematic context.
2. The ability to more intensely associate and dissociate while reenacting the problematic context.
3. Dramatization with the help of group participants can greatly emphasize the comedic aspect of the work, leading to stronger emotions.
4. Active involvement of other group members in the psychotherapy process.

We have been testing this form of therapeutic work since 2014. During seminars on provocative psychotherapy, we demonstrate provocative drama as an instrumental variation of Frank Farrelly's conventional therapeutic techniques.

Provocative Therapy Methods in Milton Erickson's Practice

Milton Erickson never used the term "provocative" to describe his methods. He is more widely known for his mastery of hypnotherapy. However, with most of his patients, he worked not through hypnosis but by applying various verbal techniques in psychotherapy, some of which embody key principles of provocative work. Erickson did not focus much on humor in psychotherapy, but occasionally used it very effectively. Like hypnosis, Erickson's humor was also highly non-directive. The essence of Erickson's various forms of work is very similar to Farrelly's approach, but the methodology may differ.

Milton Erickson

Erickson, like Farrelly, spent a considerable amount of time working in a psychiatric clinic with severely mentally ill individuals. Establishing rapport and trust with them was not always easy. However, despite this, Erickson was a master at adapting to patients, even those with severe disorders. After emotionally connecting with the patient, Erickson would then begin to provoke the desired behavior through his own actions. Erickson's therapy strategy can be described in three main points, which he applied in the vast majority of his cases.

1. Accession.
2. Leading.
3. Utilization.

Accession

At this level, the therapist begins to mimic specific verbal and non-verbal forms of the patient's behavior. This can include posture, movement, voice volume, intonation, and timbre. Connection can be established based on a person's values, beliefs, motivational patterns, action algorithms, and behavioral strategies. The therapist determines which aspect of behavior needs adjustment depending on the patient and symptoms.

Leading

Once the psychotherapist has "connected" with the patient, there is a need for them to stay in rapport with the patient at the level of mirroring their behavior. Depending on the requirements, this can range from mirroring the patient's non-verbal communication for 5–10 minutes to deeply mirroring various behavior algorithms and strategies over the course of several months. During the leading phase, the therapist is able to guide the patient's movements. The patient becomes receptive to certain recommendations from the therapist that align with their internal world. This is not yet the moment of healing, but rather a step in the direction of it.

Utilization

This stage involves the therapist carrying out a specific action or actions that reflectively exaggerate the patient's behavior while continuing to adapt and lead them. This action leads the patient to insight and sometimes catharsis. Here are a few examples of

Erickson's work that incorporate these three main principles of his practice and, in my opinion, embody the fundamental principles of provocative psychotherapeutic work.

Leslie Cameron-Bendler Case

Leslie was a very attractive girl who was accustomed to interacting with men using the language of female flirtation. Some people in her circle even called her a "flirt machine." She began attending Erickson's seminars with her friends when he was already in his seventies. During one of these seminars, she decided to test her flirting skills on Erickson and see what would happen.

Erickson noticed Leslie's flirtation and decided to "adjust" her a bit. He paused his lecture, looked intently at her, and then exclaimed, "Young lady! You must be out of your mind and in need of a psychiatrist!" He then took his left hand and lifted his right hand, which didn't work due to a long-standing illness, before letting it fall back down onto his knee. He then looked at Leslie again and said, "Even my hand doesn't get up!" Other group members laughed, Leslie blushed, and she no longer attempted to flirt with him. As one of her friends put it, she changed a bit after that, ceasing to turn almost any interaction with different men into a flirting game.

In this case, we witness Erickson's symbolic micro-adjustment through verbal pattern interruption when he exclaimed that she might need a psychiatrist, rapid pacing when he manipulated his hand, and a splendid utilization of the phrase that even his hand wouldn't lift. This serves as an excellent example of concentrated provocative work using irony and sarcasm in a nondirective manner.

Case of Jesus from the Clinic

At the clinic where Erickson worked, he was assigned to supervise a patient with schizophrenic symptoms who believed he was Jesus. Erickson pondered for a while on how to best interact with the patient, and once he had a plan, he began implementing his strategy. He went to the patient's room and asked, "Are you Jesus?" The patient replied, "Yes, of course! I am He, without a doubt!" To this, Erickson countered, "There is a carpentry job near the clinic; they are building a new wing. Are you willing to help?" The patient answered, "Certainly, I want to help people because I am a carpenter too!"

Afterward, Erickson requested, "Look, I know you're Jesus; there's no doubt about that, but other people you'll be working with may not be ready to acknowledge that. To avoid distressing them, please refer to yourself by the name and surname stated in your passport. By doing this, you'll spare them any worry." The patient thought for a while and agreed with Erickson not to reveal his "true" identity.

For the next six months, he diligently worked at the construction site, gaining a reputation as a good and helpful worker. He refrained from calling himself Jesus in front of others, which brought joy to everyone. However, in conversations with Erickson, he still considered himself as such.

After six months, the psychiatrists decided to hold a consultation to talk with the patient and observe the progression of his symptoms. They were even considering discharging him from the clinic as he had displayed excellent behavior for a prolonged period. The day before the consultation, Erickson once again asked the patient not to confess to the psychiatrists that he was indeed Jesus, so that they would release him, allowing him to freely travel the world and do good deeds.

The patient followed Erickson's advice, successfully engaged in a conversation with the psychiatrists, and was subsequently discharged. He later moved to another city, formed a community of people helping others in difficult situations, gained respect and authority within the group, and actively and successfully engaged in social volunteering. Every year on Christmas, he sent Erickson a card with greetings and a lot of gratitude for the help he had received. At the end of the letter, his real name was always written, followed by the initials J.C. (Jesus Christ).

In this case, Erickson primarily focused his attention on accessing and leading the patient. Utilization, manifested in pushing the patient to not acknowledge to other psychiatrists that he still considers himself to be Jesus, does not differ significantly from the subsequent steps. Although, to a large extent, something exaggerated in this case was simply unnecessary. It is worth noting that this work reflects the anti-psychiatric philosophy, which suggests that it is not necessary to cure the patient. It is sufficient to socially adapt them and ensure their well-being, and, as in this case, what they think of themselves and how they want to be called is irrelevant.

In my opinion, the key to constructive changes in the patient was the prolonged guidance of the patient himself. It was through this pattern that Erickson managed to "provoke" the necessary behavior. Although this form of provocation differs significantly from Farrelly's work, it demonstrates an interesting form of interaction, somewhat resembling the "devil's advocate" game of Farrelly. Erickson truly began "defending" the patient's symptom, but did so not to eliminate it but rather to place it in a more favorable social context.

Case of an Aggressive Girl

A 12-year-old girl with aggressive behavior was kept in a clinic. She would attack psychiatrists and nurses at the clinic, latching onto their hair and attempting to pull it out as soon as she had the chance. She also made attempts to tear their clothes, and when alone in her room, would rip apart the sheets and pillows.

Erickson spent some time developing a strategy for interacting with the patient. To do this, he sought the support of the clinic director and obtained permission to break some items in the girl's room for therapeutic purposes. He wanted to tear apart all the intact sheets and pillows in the room and then break the radiator off the wall.

To accomplish the latter, he asked for the heating to be turned off in her room and arranged for a nurse to stage a scene in front of the girl. When everything was prepared, he entered the girl's room. She sat on the bed, snarling angrily, ready to attack him. Erickson grabbed the items lying on the neighboring bed and vigorously and maliciously tore them apart near the girl.

He tore apart a sheet, a towel, and a pillow, emptying them of all feathers and scattering them around the room. The girl looked at him with surprise and concern. Then Erickson invited her to join him in tearing everything around them apart. She willingly joined in this total act of psychotherapeutic vandalism. When they were done with the items, Erickson asked her to help him break the radiator off the wall. They struggled with the radiator for some time until the girl gave up and it fell to the floor with a crash.

Finally, Erickson invited her to take a walk down the clinic corridor and left the room. The girl followed him hesitantly. There, they were met by a nurse, with whom Erickson had arranged to stage something in front of the girl. He ran toward the nurse, screaming angrily, then grabbed her sleeve, pulled it forcefully, and tore it off. The nurse let out a demonstrative scream. At that moment, something changed in the girl. She looked at Erickson in indignation and said, "Dr. Erickson, are you sure you can do that?"

In this case, we can see that Erickson's provocation was successful due to the strong amplification of the patient's behavior.

A splendid example of provoking the desired behavior can be seen in Erickson's work with one of his daughters. His five-year-old daughter had a habit of constantly biting her nails and could not get rid of it. No persuasions or comments from others worked.

Erickson decided to talk to her and said that for a big girl like her, it was essential to bite her nails, and one could say that nail-biting was currently her most important responsibility. Therefore, she needed to bite them regularly, every day, according to a strict schedule, precisely 15 minutes in the morning, afternoon, and evening.

At first, his daughter started following the recommendation and diligently did it for the next two weeks, but then she stopped following the schedule and stopped biting her nails.

This gentle provocation worked by reframing the context. Erickson shifted the pathological behavior into a different frame and significantly raised its significance. Erickson knew that it was easier for a little girl to get rid of what she had to do than what she wanted to do.

Understanding this method of provocation can significantly expand the technical arsenal proposed by Frank Farrelly.

Although Erickson did not always use literal humor in his

therapy, he still regarded the use of anecdotes as one of the possible ways to deliver therapeutic information to the patient.

Jeffrey Zeig writes in his book "Milton Erickson Training Seminars" that the use of anecdotes in psychotherapy can have several significant advantages.

1. Anecdotes are not threatening and do not contain threats.
2. Anecdotes provide the patient with an opportunity for enjoyment.
3. Anecdotes stimulate independent behavior since understanding and comprehending their meaning requires the individual to do so independently and make decisions based on this realization.
4. Anecdotes can be used to work with patient resistance. For example, an anecdote may contain a metaphor for action or hint at a specific meaning.
5. Anecdotes are applicable for controlling the communicative framework of relationships.
6. Anecdotes can shape a model of behavior in consciousness.
7. Anecdotes are a suggestive tool. Their use can create hypnotic confusion, thereby increasing the patient's sensitivity to hypnotic suggestion.
8. Through anecdotes, we can more easily remember the context of communication and the key meanings associated with it.

We observe a more systematic approach to studying the influence of anecdotes on the process of psychotherapy and its effectiveness.

For example, Zeig may have commented on Erickson's behavior in the following way: "Erickson had the ability to play with your attention and his own. He constantly joked, telling his stories. He intended to make you laugh and engage you in the game."

In this case, we should emphasize that for Erickson, the therapeutic process was largely associated with a state of playfulness, of which humor was an integral part. However, Erickson's humor was very subtle and veiled compared to the directive forms of irony and sarcasm characteristic of Farrelly. In my opinion, by studying the work of these two therapists, one can gain an understanding of a comprehensive approach in the practice of provocative psychotherapy, integrating both directive and non-directive methods of work. It should also be noted that Erickson was a master of creating provocative traps for patients, which he could build endlessly, unlike Farrelly, who focused on one-on-one conversations with the patient or in the presence of a group of other patients.

Pathopsychological Profiles and Provocative Psychotherapy

Hysteroid Profile

Based on our observations, hysteroid patients respond remarkably well to the influence of provocative therapeutic methods. Typically, their reactions are strong and intense. While hysteroid patients may play along with the therapist to some extent, it does not alter the essence or quality of the work. The main challenge in working with patients of this profile is navigating the traps of their excessively strong emotional reactions, which a provocative psychotherapist may inadvertently trigger. What may appear to be a powerful and intense emotion on the surface may merely be an expression of the patient's need for attention, especially in the context of group-format provocative therapy.

Paranoid Profile

It is worth noting that individuals with paranoid traits often struggle with understanding irony, sarcasm, and humor directed at them. They frequently fail to grasp the use of irony, and if they do, they begin to speculate about the therapist's motives. The favorite projections of paranoid individuals include perceiving the therapist as incompetent or making unwarranted sexual advances if the patient is of the opposite sex.

While these characteristics do not pose obstacles to provocative therapy per se, it is advisable to consider the specific nature of the patient's character and moderate the level of provocation to avoid going overboard. Initially, it is preferable to engage in a gentle approach to allow the patient to become accustomed to the therapist's communication style. More significant provocations are better introduced closer to the second half of the session.

For paranoid patients, it is highly recommended to describe the rules of provocative therapy and what the therapist intends to do in relation to the patient. Without understanding the framework of the therapeutic work, the patient may fail to perceive it as therapeutic. One of the most effective forms of provocation for patients of this profile is the "devil's advocate" technique, in which the therapist methodically, diligently, and absurdly tries to convince the paranoid individual to maintain their symptoms. Mockery and teasing aimed at this profile yield rather mediocre results.

Psychopathic Profile

Despite Frank Farrelly's claim of working with murderers and rapists in prisons, he did not provide a detailed description of what he specifically did with them. Only a few comments indicate that psychopaths appreciated his more straightforward approach. In our view, this information is too limited to generalize, as we have not personally worked with murderers and rapists in prisons using provocative psychotherapy.

However, we have encountered individuals with psychopathic personalities who are more socially adaptive, on several occasions. It is important to note that psychopathic individuals rarely seek therapy voluntarily because they believe everything is already fine with them. Sometimes, situations arise when a psychopathic person comes to therapy claiming that everything is fine, but according to their acquaintances, they should see a therapist. Such individuals do not tend to continue therapy sessions.

The psychopath's inability to experience guilt and shame makes them challenging subjects for provocative therapy. Being in a passive position, being controlled, having therapy conducted on them, or being provoked contradicts their predatory nature. In our work with psychopaths, we found that their psychological essence responds weakly to provocative work. Although the results may vary depending on the individual, we frequently receive consistent feedback from individuals of this profile that provocations simply do not affect them, even when they are highly sophisticated.

We do not analyze the long-term effects of provocative therapy with psychopathic personalities since they usually do not stay in therapy for an extended period and are inclined to downplay any impact the therapist may have on them. In the short-term form of work, the therapeutic effect we observed was minimal. However, similar weak effects of verbal psychotherapy are observed in all other schools of psychotherapy. We have not found any examples of any psychotherapy approach claiming to successfully correct psychopathy in any form.

Obsessive-Compulsive Profile

According to my observations, this profile responds excellently to the influence of provocative therapy, and various techniques can be effective. The "devil's advocate" technique and harsh mockery of symptoms can be particularly beneficial. I have not encountered strong resistance or rejection of this form of therapy from patients.

Schizoid Profile

When working with this personality profile, it is necessary to dose the provocative therapeutic "poison." This is because behind the coldness and lack of emotions of the schizoid individual often lies a very sensitive and vulnerable person. During the therapeutic process, it is important to take note of the level of irony and sarcasm that the patient can tolerate.

Schizoid individuals are narcissistic and extremely sensitive to any jokes directed at themselves. This should be taken into account to achieve a therapeutic effect and not simply provoke and further close off the patient. If the patient's narcissism is too pronounced, the optimal approach would be to focus on the "devil's advocate" technique, in which the therapist absurdly attempts to support the symptom and convince the patient to maintain it. Provocative psychotherapy has proven to be highly effective in working with patients of this profile.

Epileptoid Profile

Epileptoid patients generally respond well to provocative work and do not exhibit strong resistance to it. The intensity of provocation may need to be adjusted based on the individual. However, most of these patients tolerate moderate and high levels of provocation quite well.

The main challenge may arise when working with epilepsy patients with low levels of intelligence. They often fail to understand mild irony and may take offense at harsh sarcasm, rarely benefiting from such provocation.

Schizophrenic Profile

Farrelly repeatedly described and commented on the excellent effects of provocative work on schizophrenic patients. It can temporarily bring them to a relatively normal state. Similar effects have been observed not only in schizophrenic patients but also in individuals with a schizoid accent in their personalities. Absurdity, irony, and sarcasm directed at individuals with this profile can effectively balance and regulate their behavior.

Manic-Depressive Profile

Patients with this profile generally respond well to provocative therapy. However, their reactions can significantly vary depending on the phase of manic-depressive dynamic they are in.

During the manic phase, patients may excessively engage in a comedic and humorous context of therapy, losing their serious approach to the process. It is preferable to avoid this situation, as it can sharply reduce the effectiveness of therapy. The patient should be aware of what they are engaging in. Otherwise, the therapy's effectiveness will decline.

Ideally, meeting the patient during the interphase, where neither manic nor depressive states dominate, is excellent. In the depressive phase, there may be difficulties with normal reactions to the therapist's jokes. During this period, the patient's sense of humor may temporarily diminish.

However, In my opinion, this is not a contraindication for provocative therapeutic work.

A Brief Message from the Author

Mastering complex psychotherapeutic theories and practices can be a challenging journey. By sharing your experience with this book, you can guide others who are on the same path. Your review could inspire someone to take the next step in deepening their knowledge and applying these insights to make meaningful changes in their life.

Thank you for your support and for taking the time to share your thoughts! Your feedback helps us refine our offerings and empowers others in their pursuit of mastering psychotherapy. If this book has been valuable to you, I'd be grateful if you could take a moment to leave a review. **Your positive rating would mean a lot!**

To share your feedback, simply scan the QR code or click the link below:

psychemaster.com/recommends/review-provocative-therapy

Bibliography

1. Seminar with Dr. Milton H. Erickson: Lessons in Hypnosis. Edited and commented by J.K. Zeig. Moscow: Independent Firm "Klass," 1994.
2. Radin, P. Trickster: A Study of North American Indian Myths with Comments by C.G. Jung and C.C. Kerenyi. St. Petersburg: Eurasia, 1999, pp. 265-286.
3. Farrelly, F., and Brandsma, D. Provocative Therapy. Moscow: Publishing House "Ekaterinburg," 1996.
4. Haley, J. About Milton Erickson. Translated by V.M. Sarina and Y.A. Khudokon. Moscow: Independent Firm "Klass," 1998.
5. Erickson, M.G. The February Man: Hypnotherapy and the Development of Self-Awareness. Milton H. Erickson, Ernest L. Rossi; translated by E.L. Dlugach. Moscow: Independent Firm "Klass," 1995.
6. Erickson, M. Hypnotic Realities: Induction of Clinical Hypnosis and Forms of Indirect Suggestion. Milton Erickson, Ernest Rossi, and Sheila Rossi; translated by M.A. Yakushina, edited by M.R. Ginzburg. Moscow: Klass, 2000.
7. Erickson, M. The Strategy of Psychotherapy: Selected Works. Authorized translation and editing by L.M. Shlionsky. St. Petersburg: Rech, 2002.
8. Erickson, M. Teaching Seminar with Dr. Milton H. Erickson,

M.D.: Lessons in Hypnosis. Edited and commented by Jeffrey K. Zeig; translated by T.K. Kruglova. Moscow: Klass, 2003.

About the Author

Dr. **Artem Kudelia**, a psychologist with a PhD and a practicing therapist, has extensive expertise in integrative approaches. He possesses comprehensive knowledge of a wide range of psychotherapeutic methods, including humanistic and existential theories, as well as the practical application of cognitive-behavioral therapy (CBT) to effectively address issues such as anxiety, depression, obsessive thoughts, compulsions, social phobias, and complex emotions. His books are valuable resources for professionals and individuals interested in managing their mental health. In addition to managing symptoms, he helps his clients toward self-actualization in various aspects of their lives, including social, career, and personal aspects.

You can connect with me on:

- 🔗 https://facebook.com/psyche.masters
- 🔗 https://instagram.com/psyche.masters
- 🔗 https://threads.net/@psyche.masters
- 🔗 https://youtube.com/@psyche.masters
- 🔗 https://tiktok.com/@psyche.masters
- 🔗 https://pinterest.com/psychemasters

Subscribe to my newsletter:

✉ https://psychemaster.com/early-reader-signup

Also by Artem Kudelia PhD

The ***Psychology & Psychotherapy Theories & Practices*** series offers a detailed examination of the history, theoretical foundations, and practical applications of fundamental approaches in psychotherapy. It is an indispensable resource for psychologists, medical professionals, psychology students, and anyone interested in understanding these complex subjects.

Additionally, the ***Cognitive Behavioral Therapy Self-Help Guide: 15 Steps to Mental Health*** series provides actionable guidance for overcoming various psychological challenges, such as anxiety, depression, excessive anger, obsessive thoughts, compulsions, social phobias, health anxiety, and intricate emotional struggles. These topics were chosen because many individuals facing these challenges often lack awareness of the underlying dynamics. By gaining insight into these processes, individuals can make informed decisions about seeking help, reinforcing the idea that knowledge is a powerful tool for personal empowerment.

Together, these series offer invaluable resources for those interested in psychology, whether for academic study or personal development, by providing comprehensive insights and practical tools that contribute to improved mental well-being.

Psychotherapy Fundamentals Complete Guide

Are you struggling to understand complex psychotherapeutic theories?

Psychotherapy Fundamentals: Complete Guide simplifies the intricate world of psychotherapy, making it accessible and actionable for those interested in self-discovery, self-education, and readers with a wide range of interests.

♥ Imagine confidently navigating psychotherapeutic real-world scenarios with ease.

This book is your *comprehensive roadmap to achieving a deep and practical understanding of psychotherapy.* You'll learn to simplify complex theories and integrate them effectively into your life and practice.

Gain a comprehensive understanding of various therapeutic approaches, including *provocative* therapy, *humanistic* therapy, *somatic* therapy, *existential* therapy, *drama* therapy, *psychedelic* and *post-psychedelic* therapy, *anti-psychiatric* therapy, and *integrative* therapy. Each chapter delves into the key themes and methods of these psychotherapy modalities, broadening the horizons for those interested in self-discovery, self-education, and lifelong learning.

▼

https://books2read.com/Psychotherapy-Fundamentals

Hypnotherapy Fundamentals Complete Guide

Are you ready to uncover the secrets of hypnotherapy?

This comprehensive guide immerses you in the ***theory*** *and history of hypnosis*, providing a solid foundation for understanding the principles underlying hypnotherapy.

Explore the various techniques and approaches used in *hypnotherapy* ***training*** through ***practice exercises***, including the art of *suggestion* and deepening *hypnotic trance states*, the creation of therapeutic propositions, and the utilization of the power of the subconscious mind.

Learn how to effectively apply *hypnotherapy techniques* to address a wide range of issues, from managing stress and anxiety to overcoming phobias and habits.

Gain an understanding of the transformative potential of hypnosis and its applications for personal growth and well-being.

Unlock the secrets of harnessing the power of the mind and creating positive changes in yourself and others.

https://books2read.com/Hypnotherapy-Fundamentals

Psychology of Love & Death
Therapeutic Path to Fundamental Balance in Life and Relationships

How to Achieve Fundamental Balance in Life and Relationships?

Explore dualistic nature of human consciousness, along with the profound impact of seeking balance between fundamental continuums of *love and death*, *instinct and spirituality*, *masculinity and femininity* in shaping our experiences and relationships.

Explore the psychopathological profiles and manifestations of love and death, including profiles such as hysteria, paranoia, psychopathy, and others.

Uncover different types of love, from eros to agape, and study the *three-component Theory of Love.*

Familiarize yourself with *real-life psychotherapy cases* that illustrate the complexities of love, death, and therapy and gain *valuable insights* into the human experience and its challenges.

https://books2read.com/Psychology-of-Love-and-Death

Breathwork Therapy Seminar
Holotropic Journey to Unconscious Mind Secrets

Tap Into the Wisdom of Transpersonal Psychology!

This book is the transcript of a seminar that addresses the profound questions of *subconsciousness*, offering a unique perspective on personal growth and healing.

Gain profound insights into the workings of your mind and explore the mysteries of human consciousness.

Access practical exercises and *techniques* to facilitate personal growth, healing, and self-awareness through *breathwork.*

Written for seekers of self-awareness, psychology enthusiasts, and anyone curious about the depths of the human mind.

Explore the integration of spirituality and psychology, uncovering your inner potential.

▼

https://books2read.com/Breathwork-Therapy

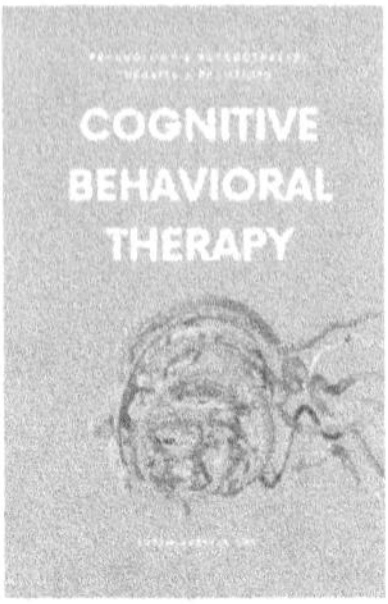

Cognitive Behavioral Therapy
Managing Anxiety and Depression

Explore the roots of anxiety and learn why it's a fundamental aspect of the human experience.

An in-depth exploration of *Panic Disorder*, addressing the irrational fears associated with it.

Examine the nuances of *Social Anxiety* and its impact on personal and professional spheres.

Dive into the world of *Obsessive-Compulsive Disorder*, unraveling its complexities.

Understand the genetic predispositions and learn effective strategies to manage obsessions and compulsions.

Explore *PTSD* from its roots to its biological manifestations. Delve into the trauma cycles, and discover therapeutic techniques for stabilization and overcoming trauma.

Grasp the degrees of *Depression*, from mild to severe, debunking common myths.

https://books2read.com/Cognitive-Behavioral-Therapy

Psychotherapy
Introduction to Healing Vectors

Do you want to understand the variety of methods of psychotherapy and choose the one that is best for you?

In the vast world of psycho-technologies, there are numerous methods of psychotherapy that encompass a wide range of *personality theories* and concepts.

Drawing upon an integral framework, the book maps out the complex *landscape of psychotherapy*, encompassing vectors such as *psychoanalytic*, *hypnotic*, *provocative*, *humanistic*, *behavioral*, *existential*, *transpersonal*, *cognitive*, *somatic*, *psychodramatic* and *psychedelic* therapies, among many others.

This book will provide you with valuable knowledge that will allow you to choose the most suitable therapeutic path for specific circumstances and personality types.

https://books2read.com/Psychotherapy-Introduction

Humanistic Therapy
From Crisis to Self-Actualization

Do you want to explore a world where people are seen as unique holistic systems with infinite potential waiting to be discovered?

Immerse yourself in the theories and practices of humanistic therapy and explore the *transformative path from crisis to self-actualization.*

Unlike psychoanalysis, which focuses on internal complexes and personal traumas, humanistic therapy emphasizes the *study and development of positive personality qualities.*

Humanistic philosophy has also influenced fields such as *education*, promoting *empathy* and *support* as the foundation of learning.

This holistic approach recognizes the *interconnectedness of mind, body, and spirit* and seeks to stimulate personal *growth* and *well-being.*

Take the first step towards self-awareness, personal growth, and a more fulfilling existence.

https://books2read.com/Humanistic-Therapy

Somatic Therapy
The Wisdom of the Body

Would you like to establish a connection with your body and access the source of wisdom?

Unleash the transformative power of *somatic therapy* and embark on a journey of *self-discovery* and *healing.*

Explore the profound connection between the *mind and body.*

Discover the *seven levels of muscular armor* and their connection to specific emotions such as sadness, anger, and fear.

By exploring different body segments, you will unlock *powerful techniques* for releasing pent-up emotions and promoting harmony throughout the organism. From *eye movements* and *jaw exercises* to *deep breathing* and *body movements*, this book offers *practical methods* for *accessing the wisdom of the body* and *restoring emotional balance.*

Acquire unique knowledge about *healing after birth trauma and psychosomatic medicine.*

https://books2read.com/Somatic-Therapy

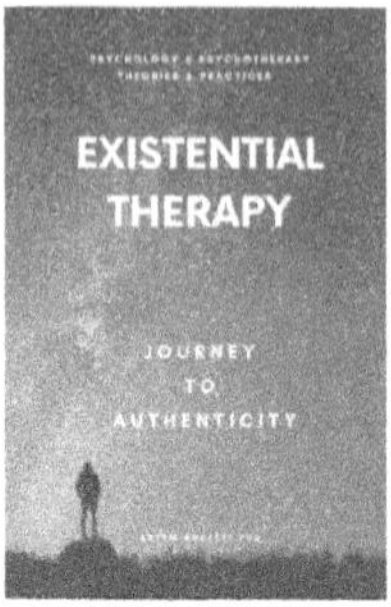

Existential Therapy
Journey to Authenticity

Do you want to know who you really are? What is your personal meaning of existence?

Embark on a *transformative journey* to uncover your *true essence* and embrace the *principles* of existential therapy.

Explore the rich philosophical roots of *existential psychotherapy* and find your path to *personal authenticity.*

Explore key themes such as *freedom, responsibility, meaning,* and *choice*, and learn to courageously and authentically navigate the complexities of existence.

This book provides *practical ideas and techniques* for *applying the principles of existential therapy* to your own life.

Gain a deep *understanding* of your *values, beliefs*, and *desires*, and learn to *embrace uncertainty* and *transform* life's *challenges* into *opportunities* for *growth* and *self-discovery.*

https://books2read.com/Existential-Therapy

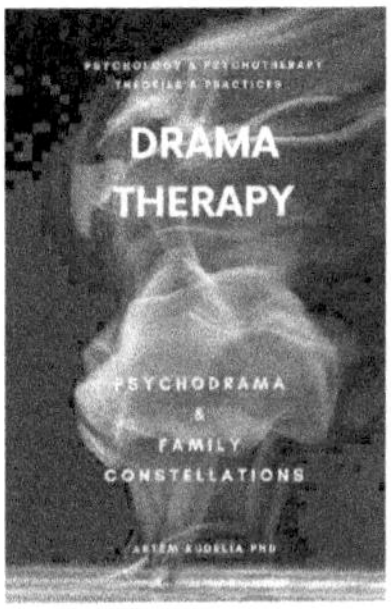

Drama Therapy
Potential of Psychodrama and Family Constellations

Explore the unique world of drama therapeutic approach!

Therapeutic model of intervention that encompasses 12 *powerful speech patterns* capable of significantly *influencing conscious and unconscious processes.*

Through *psychodramatic techniques* and *family constellations*, you will *gain practical knowledge* to enhance your therapeutic practice.

Addressing a wide spectrum of *psychopathological profiles*, including *hysteria, paranoia*, and *obsessive-compulsive disorders*, this book equips you with effective dramatherapeutic activities and psychodynamic exercises.

It serves as a *comprehensive guide* to *crisis intervention, counseling theory*, and *strategies for addiction rehabilitation.*

Gain an understanding of the right hemisphere and the *neuroscience* underlying drama therapy, and learn to *navigate complex emotional situations* with *understanding* and *acceptance.*

▽

https://books2read.com/Drama-Therapy-Constellations

Psychedelic Therapy
The Healing Power Therapeutic Journeys

Embark on a transformative journey into the world of psychedelic therapy!

Explore the fascinating *history* of *psychedelic substances* and potential benefits of working with consciousness-altering substances in clinical practice.

Learn comprehensive information on various *psychedelic therapies*, including *ketamine therapy*, *psilocybin*-assisted psychotherapy, *MDMA*-assisted psychotherapy, and *ibogaine* psychotherapy.

Gain knowledge about *mental health* in the *perinatal period*, the *role of hypnosis*, and the transformative power of *holotropic breathwork.*

Understand the profound impact of *psychedelic medicine* and the potential of *psilocybin microdosing.*

Explore the therapeutic applications of *ketamine* in the *treatment of depression* and *psychosynthesis in coaching.*

https://books2read.com/Psychedelic-Therapy-Journey

Beyond Psychiatry
Exploring Anti-Psychiatry Method

Challenge traditional psychiatry and psychotherapy!

This book presents an *alternative to conventional* ideas of normalcy and offers a *fresh perspective on psychological disorders*, inviting readers to question existing paradigms.

Delve deeper into *psychopathological profiles* and *anti-psychiatric* forms of psychotherapy, examining various profiles including *hysteria, paranoia, psychopathy*, and more.

Gain an understanding of the intersection of psychotherapy and existential philosophy, *challenging the myth of mental illness* within families.

Explore the *treatment of psychosis, trauma*, and *emotional disorders from a holistic perspective*.

https://books2read.com/Beyond-Psychiatry

Integrative Therapy
Personal Transformation Guide

Discover the Power of Integrative Therapy and Embark on a Journey of Personal Transformation!

This book challenges traditional divisions in *therapeutic approaches* and explores the potential of *combining multiple vectors* to create a *comprehensive and integrated therapeutic system.*

Immerse yourself in the world of *neuro-linguistic programming* (NLP), *cognitive styles, neurological levels*, and *integral philosophy*, among other concepts.

Explore practical methodologies such as *shifting negative thinking*, *creating rapport*, and using linguistic patterns to facilitate positive change.

Unlock the transformative *power of anchors*, *changing personal history* and *submodalities.*

Gain an understanding of maps of the world and the *metamodel* for *effective communication.*

▼

https://books2read.com/Integrative-Therapy

Theory & History of Hypnosis
Exploring Altered State of Mind in Trance

Immerse yourself in the fascinating world of hypnosis and explore the history and theory of altered states of consciousness!

This book sheds light on *historical trance practices* and the *role of shamanism*, tracing its influence on *modern psychospiritual orientations.*

Discover the benefits of this book by exploring the *history of trance practices and hypnotherapy.*

Explore the *evolution* of *shamanism*, its connection to *religion*, and its pre-religious *philosophy*, which offered deep insights into the structure of the universe and the mysteries of the spiritual world.

Discover various *hypnotic phenomena* and *states of consciousness* that can be induced in a trance state.

Explore their potential applications in *psychotherapeutic practice*, from *pain management* to the *treatment of depression.*

Learn techniques such as *self-hypnosis, deep trance induction*, and *guided healing visualizations.*

https://books2read.com/Theory-and-History-of-Hypnosis

Hypnotherapy Training
A Guide for Practicing Hypnotherapists

Uncover the secrets of hypnotherapy and improve your practical hypnosis skills!

This book explores *techniques* and *practical skills* for hypnotherapists.

Dive into the depths of the *subconscious* and discover the *transformative potential* of hypnotherapy.

Discover the benefits of this book, which delves into key topics and approaches in *hypnotherapy training.*

Explore developed techniques, including rapport-building practices and the use of matching postures, movements, and breathing with the client.

Engage in exercises that enable the attainment of different trance levels and explore the motives of trance and their application in psychotherapy.

Gain an understanding of different styles and orientations of hypnotic work, from hypnoanalytic and suggestive to behavioral and transpersonal.

https://books2read.com/Hypnotherapy-Training

Healing Anxiety and Overthinking
Proven CBT Strategies for Lasting Relief

Are you exhausted from the relentless cycle of anxiety and overthinking?

Discover the 15-step program that will transform your mental health and bring peace of mind.

Millions of adults struggle with anxiety and overthinking, feeling trapped in a cycle of worry and stress. But it doesn't have to be this way. "*Healing Anxiety and Overthinking: Proven CBT Strategies for Lasting Relief*" offers a comprehensive guide to breaking free from the grip of anxiety using practical, proven **Cognitive Behavioral Therapy** (**CBT**) strategies.

♥ ***Imagine waking up every day with a clear mind, free from the constant barrage of anxious thoughts***

This book is your roadmap to achieving that transformation in just 15 steps. You'll learn to understand the nature of your anxiety, identify its triggers, and apply effective techniques to manage and overcome it.

Take Control of Your Mental Health

Don't let anxiety and overthinking rule your life. With "*Healing Anxiety and Overthinking,*" you'll gain the tools and confidence to achieve peace of mind and live the life you deserve.

Mastering Intrusive Thoughts
Practical CBT Techniques for Managing OCD

*Is **OCD** ruling your life with intrusive thoughts and compulsions?*

Take back control with scientifically-proven CBT techniques designed to help you regain peace of mind.

Millions of adults struggle with obsessive-compulsive disorder (OCD), caught in a relentless cycle of intrusive thoughts and compulsive behaviors. "Mastering Intrusive Thoughts" is your step-by-step guide to breaking free from the grip of OCD using practical, evidence-based Cognitive Behavioral Therapy (CBT) techniques.

♥ ***Picture yourself waking up with a calm, focused mind, no longer burdened by the constant anxiety of unwanted thoughts.***

In this book, Dr. Artem Kudelia offers a clear and actionable path to mastering your thoughts in 15 manageable steps. Whether you're new to CBT or have tried other methods without success, this guide provides the tools you need to finally achieve relief.

✔ **Take the First Step Towards Mental Freedom**

You'll gain the knowledge and confidence to conquer your **OCD** and reclaim your peace of mind.

The Anger Solution
A CBT Program for Emotional Balance

Are you tired of living with persistent anger and overwhelming stress?

Discover a practical, 15-step program designed to bring lasting peace and transform your emotional health.

Millions of adults struggle with anger and stress, feeling trapped in a cycle of frustration and tension. But it doesn't have to be this way. "The Anger Solution" offers a comprehensive guide to breaking free from the grip of anger using practical, proven Cognitive Behavioral Therapy (CBT) strategies.

♥ ***Imagine waking up every day with a calm mind, free from the constant barrage of anger and stress.***

This book is your roadmap to achieving that transformation. With clear, actionable steps, you'll learn to understand the nature of your anger, identify its triggers, and apply effective techniques to manage and overcome it.

✔ **Take Control of Your Emotional Health**

With "The Anger Solution," you'll gain the tools and confidence to achieve emotional balance and live the life you deserve.

Health Anxiety Mastery
30 Proven CBT Steps to Peace of Mind

Is health anxiety controlling your life with constant worry and fear?

Regain peace of mind with proven CBT techniques designed to help you overcome health-related anxiety and reclaim control.

Millions of people struggle with health anxiety, trapped in a cycle of physical symptoms, endless reassurance-seeking, and intrusive thoughts about their well-being. *"Health Anxiety Mastery"* offers a clear, step-by-step approach to breaking free from these patterns using practical, evidence-based Cognitive Behavioral Therapy (CBT) techniques.

♥ **Imagine waking up each day calm and confident, no longer overwhelmed by fear and obsessive thoughts about your health.**

In this book, you'll find 30 actionable steps to help you reduce anxiety, challenge limiting beliefs, and develop healthier thought patterns. Whether you're just beginning your journey or have tried other approaches without success, these practical tools will guide you toward lasting relief.

✔ **Start Your Journey to Balanced Mental Health**

With *"Health Anxiety Mastery,"* you'll discover how to transform fear into empowerment and take control of your well-being once and for all.

How to Get Over Social Anxiety
CBT Strategies for True Confidence and Deep Connection

What if 15 proven steps could free you from social anxiety and help you connect?

Uncover a 15-step CBT program to overcome fear, stop avoidance, and build true self-confidence. Millions struggle with social anxiety, but you don't have to face it alone. This guide provides a clear, evidence-based path to transforming your social life and connecting authentically.

♥ **Imagine engaging in conversations fearlessly and forming genuine relationships free from judgment or rejection.**

With insights from proven cognitive-behavioral techniques and relatable examples, this book offers the practical tools and encouragement needed to face your fears and succeed socially.

✔ **Begin Your Journey to Confidence**

Start transforming fear into connection and reclaim control of your social life with "*How to Get Over Social Anxiety*."

Discover More by Artem Kudelia

Scan the QR code or click the link to access his author page and full collection. Each book provides detailed insights and practical guidance, exemplifying his contributions to psychology and psychotherapy.

books2read.com/Artem-Kudelia-PhD

www.ingramcontent.com/pod-product-compliance
Lightning Source LLC
La Vergne TN
LVHW022017200926
848481LV00007B/2443
* 9 7 9 8 2 3 0 0 1 3 2 2 8 *